DON'T TOUCH THE BONES

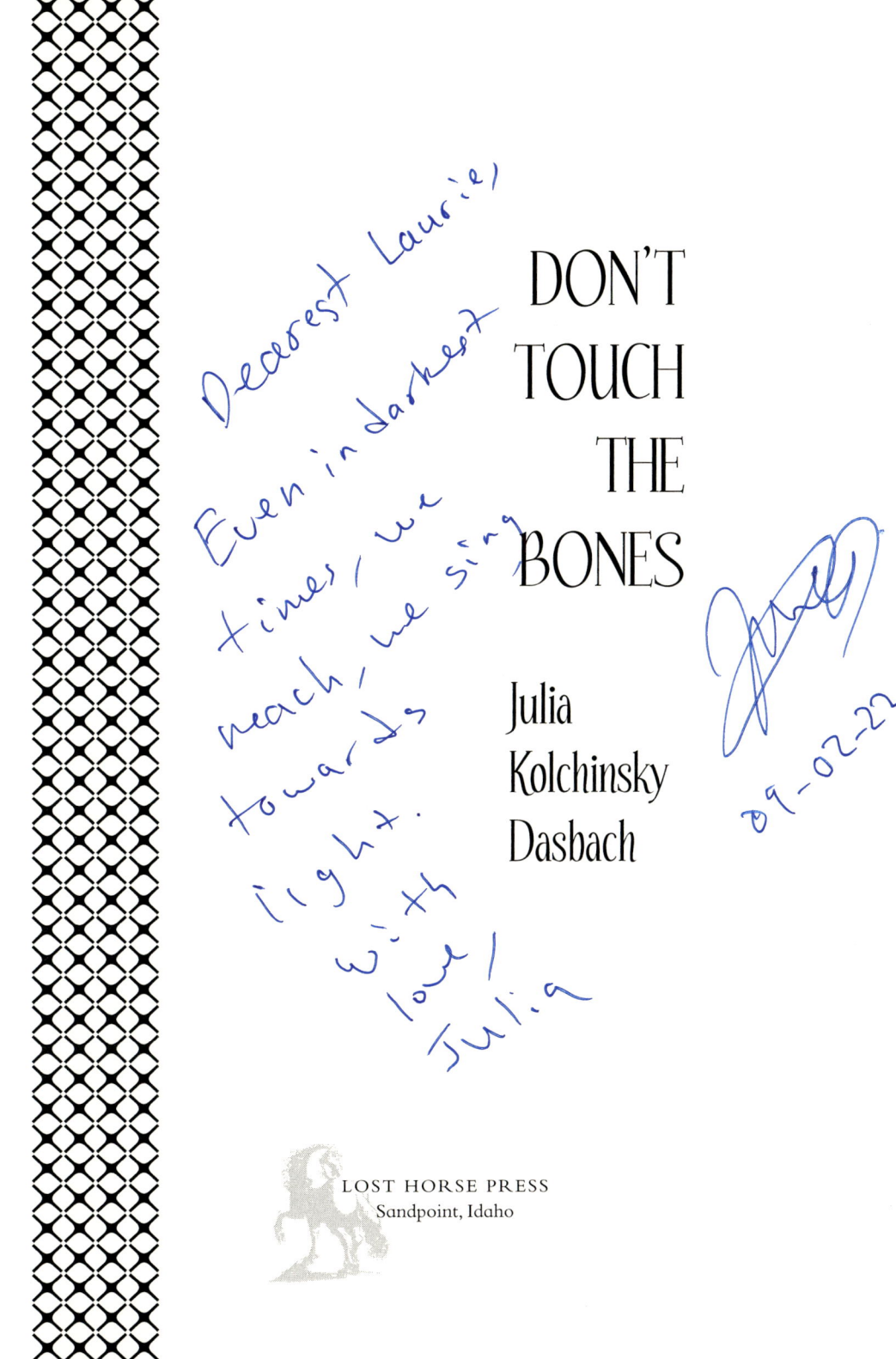

DON'T
TOUCH
THE
BONES

Julia
Kolchinsky
Dasbach

Dearest Laurie/
Even in darkest
times, we
reach, we sing
towards
light.
with
love/
Julia

09-02-22

LOST HORSE PRESS
Sandpoint, Idaho

Author Photo: Kenneth Dasbach.
Book Design: Christine Holbert.

FIRST EDITION

This and other fine Lost Horse Press titles may be viewed online at www.losthorsepress.org.

LIBRARY OF CONGRESS CATALOGING-IN-PUBLICATION DATA
    Cataloging-in-Publication Data may be obtained from the Library of Congress..
    ISBN 978-1-7333400-2-1

Моей семье
For my family

Memory creates the chain of tradition
which passes a happening from generation to generation . . .
It starts the web which all stories together form in the end.

—*Walter Benjamin,* "The Storyteller"

In memory of my great-grandparents,
Vikhlya Moshka-Gershkovna Khalfin
& Simon Mordakovich Barash

Of Holocaust victims and survivors,
named and unnamed

Table of Contents

Foreword

TWENTY YEARS AGO, HISTORIAN PETER NOVICK wrote provocatively, in *The Holocaust in American Life,* that "[m]ourning and remembering the dead are, of course, traditional Jewish obligations. But Judaism has consistently disparaged excessive or prolonged mourning." Novick was warning against placing the Shoah at the center of American Jewish identity, of fetishizing suffering in a way that he characterized as "un-Jewish." In her latest collection, *Don't Touch the Bones,* Julia Dasbach demonstrates her deep awareness of such concerns and offers a poetry—post-Auschwitz, post-Adorno—that refuses to fetishize atrocity and that is profoundly Jewish in its examination of sustained, intergenerational grief.

A scholar of Holocaust literature, Dasbach is extremely knowledgeable of the historiography and the critical theory of the field. She brings a scholar's sensibilities to her poems, frequently demonstrating how her work enters a multinational, multilingual, multi-generational, and interdisciplinary conversation about the aesthetic challenges of representing the Shoah on the page. The book engages with poems by Russian writers like Anna Akhmatova, Osip Mandelstam, Aleksander Pushkin, and Alexander Rozenbaum, addressing these poets as if they are intimate acquaintances, family members. Indeed, the poet, whose own family came to the United States in the early 1990s as part of the post-Soviet exodus of Ukrainian Jewry, has maintained an intimate connection to her mothertongue and to the landscape of Ukraine, a country of potatoes and summer nights without darkness and the ravine known as Babi Yar. In formally compelling poems such as "Ghazal Refusing to Name the Holocaust," "Misremembering Stones," and "Driftwood Pantoum," Dasbach demonstrates it is at the place where American, Ukrainian, and Jewish identities intersect that she can offer powerful insights about the transmission of trauma across generations, the manner in which privilege shifts depending on one's geography, and the Shoah's continuing relevance to our current moment.

Ultimately, *Don't Touch the Bones* argues that the Shoah remains everywhere. The very bones of this horror are to be found not only as real fragments buried in the earth, but they also exist in the air, in the fire, the water, the aether, and even in our very own bodies. The speaker in these poems often expresses her worries as a mother of a young child.

If the Shoah is contained within her, passed down through the generations—the way some families might carry the traits of red hair or blue eyes—what will she pass on to her own child? Even though her son is only a toddler, she recognizes that she has already begun "teaching him / the endlessness of bones."

The bones are memory, trauma, history. "We don't know how / to know such things," Dasbach writes, by which she means the vast numbers of the murdered, who they were, how they continue to reside inside of us. But, even if we don't know how to know such things, Dasbach's poems seem to assert that an attempt at knowledge has its own kind of meaning and even a painful, disconcerting beauty. In "Family Portrait as a Collection of Bones," the speaker is warned by her grandmother to resist the impulse to collect:

> She tells me not to look
>
> for bones, that collection amounts
> to very little and the man who collected
> millions of light bulbs
>
>   still died
> in a museum of glass, outlived
> by his assembled light.

Yes, the poet is saying, these poems of mine, these artful groupings of bones, may end up in a brittle museum. But at least they are displayed together and glittering exquisitely in the wounded light of language.

—*Jehanne Dubrow*

Hyoid Bone Kaddish

My people know how to hold light
in their mouths, how to keep it safe

until it fades to whisper or prayer.
Now say: *Amen*

until you can tell the difference.
My people are light and bone

and when god opened his mouth
to say: *Amen*

they must have leapt off his tongue,
unchosen and nameless

beyond any blessing and song.

I IN THE EARTH

They used to pour millet on graves or poppy seeds
To feed the dead who would come disguised as birds.
I put this book here for you, who once lived
So that you should visit us no more.

—Czeslaw Milosz, "Dedication"

Take a piece of earth

We will not allow the building of anything on bones of people.

—Governor Alexander Rogachuk, Belarus
DailyMailUK, "Mass grave containing 1,000 executed
Jewish men, women, and children uncovered"

see all two-hundred
& seventy bones found at birth
in a single body. Multiply each
by a thousand, ten-thousand,
hundred-thousand, million
by the millions. Magnitude
past numbers, beyond
bodies. We don't know how
to know such things.
We try to take them
in our hands. Sift the soil
we let our children
build on, palming dirt
into their open mouths.
Wash their hands of it.
Scrub under the nails.
We still can't clean
what gets inside.
Show me a place
not made of bone
& see the generations
we have swallowed.

Family Portrait as a Collection of Bones

My dog collects bones, buries them
in couch cushions as though they were
the earth, returning to find them

whole and uneaten by worms.
My husband collects bruises, counts
how many rise above the skin, how wide

the purpling icebergs spread. He collects
bass strings, forms them into hanging loops,
bronzing nooses. My father collects

words, reading everything and hiding
sunflower seeds in his pockets
so he can chew and smile without having

to speak. He collects centuries and kingdoms
in a world where he is warrior and lord
and matters. My mother, she collects

collecting, keeps my room a mausoleum, missing
only the body. Grandfather collects replicas
of himself: a chess player, a head of hair,

a lesson of how to clean the countertop
with baking soda and a steady hand.
Grandmother collects children,

grandchildren and their worry, buries it deep
inside her chest as though it were
the earth. She tells me not to look

for bones, that collection amounts
to very little and the man who collected
millions of light bulbs

                                  still died
in a museum of glass, outlived
by his assembled light.

Don't touch the bones.

after Rachel (Mutterperl) Goldfarb

stop writing the same story.
the winter corn is already high,
    she says. cast-iron skillets, brass teapots
and wedding bands thaw to bullets,
    but his name is still missing.

"this I remember distinctly" repeats:
    there was a clearing, calling mother's
name, there was a clearing, they started to shoot.
    the winter corn was already high,
as she told the same story.

    the priest would take matzo and give
her honey in return, call her my child and stay
    blind to her origin, cast in
iron skillets and brass teapots
    where his name is still missing.

she married an Auschwitz survivor
    without a number. he lies
about remembering the gravestone streets
    where her wedding band would thaw
to bullets, writing the same story.

    they're unearthing mass graves now.
in Ukraine, Poland, Hungry, and all that was
    united once. they're counting bones
and writing that same story, but
    my great-grandfather's name stays missing.

Out of Stone

Treblinka Memorial Park

the smell of eggs and herring. so much
stone, I considered bringing a small one back
to my great-grandmother's grave. but she'd had
enough already. enough of Eastern Europe.
enough of weight. of stone. it must all be
stone made of stones where she is. boulders really.
some embossed. some charred. some loved
with rocks or dry flowers or tea
candles. some just with wax
and others with flags. some,
so far, who would endure
how long it takes
to get to loving them?
and who loves
a stone?

the loved
turn into or out of it.
stone to black
moth. petrified. the cleft
of a river. stone out of
stone out of uneven cobble.
cobble to asphalt and uneven
love and unleavened
bread. taste of stone. linger
tasteless. evergreens
needle this gray ground an acid
red. acrid stones
that smell only
if you listen close.

II IN THE AIR

Этот воздух пусть будет свидетелем—
Let this air be a witness—

—Osip Mandelstam, "Verses on an Unknown Soldier"

In Praise of Forgetting

Forget to turn off the lights and wash the dishes and empty the tub.

Forget the standing water and let it bring ghosts into the house.

Forget street numbers and front doors and languages of all the ones
    you've lived in before.

Forget the names you gave them once. How they were taken way.

Forget home is where the heart is. The heart can't beat outside the body.

Forget the body. Theirs. Forget they are made of water. Standing.

Forget to lie down. And forget to sleep. It's too quiet in these walls.

Forget the four walls and the hands it took to build them.

Forget hands. How it felt to press palm to ribcage to the stove.

Forget to light it.

Forget how the cold and blueless dark make outlines of ghosts glow
    a harvest moon.

Forget the moon. It doesn't belong here. Here ghosts are houses inside
    of houses.

Songs of Home

I. To My Sister Anna
after Akhmatova

Sister, how could you recognize   my new earth-mother then,
since you were *not*   *with those who left the land?*
My songs are not for them, you said   and kept on singing
sinking   on your knees   into your own frost-covered
bearer, Mother Russia,   mother of the mounting dead.
How could America and I   discover harmony
in an English tongue, the one   more native to me now
than the blood that binds   the two of us   to a once
so solid   sacred   Soviet ground?

You sang to us:

> *Confusion occupies the world,*
> *and I am powerless to tell*
> *somebody brute from something human.*

I wonder if you saw   the blocks of ice   they hurled at those once marked
by stars and now   just by familiar features.   Did you watch
as they traded skin   for goldfinch-plume   grew more red
around the eyes   keeping the yellow hidden
on the underside of sharp black wings   so only as they flew away
could the frozen ground see   who was abandoning her.

Do not blame or pity me   dear Sister,   for joining
those you are against   for the golden flight   I chose
but in the way of your own faith   *Say a prayer for me*
so I may find a way back   *to our ruined home*   where you and I
can sing together

                    for your voice has rung   in every mouth

across your Mother Russia, and in mine   it sinks   stinging   my gums
like the splintering crust of stale bread   turned to ice.
Your music   won't take shape here   on this foreign coast
that hasn't bled enough   to know the weight
of your *last toast.*   But Sister, let me unclench   my jaw for you
No, not mine. It's someone else's wound,   show you my teeth
are rutted, stained   red like the frozen Neva you once described
its blooming bonfires   on my tongue   which can still learn
the ease of memory   like yours   it's been crushed down
by the crunch of bloodstained boots   and like yourself
when asked   *"Can you describe this?"*   my tongue
has answered,   *"Yes, I can."*   only
using English words   thinking Soviet thoughts   bleeding
                                                    Jewish blood.

II. To My Brother Osip

after Mandelstam

On this warmer foreign ground   I think of how your music

fell as snow   unclothing all your poems   of the wilder furs

that once warmed those   who should have walked

barefoot   along your trail

while you sang:

> *I want to leave*
>
> *the Russian language.*

But dear Brother, the Cyrillic song leapt off your tongue

before you could learn   to make melody   in another

and on the page you left only   skinned and hollowed

bones: a frostbitten mirror of what you would become

in the undiscovered

> Siberian white.

Dear Brother, they tried to freeze your lips   lose your body

in the dry tangle of steppe   but you sparked on

like wet-wood bursts   and wrapped in ice you called yourself

a double-dealer with a double soul   so even when they turned you cold

one part of you   would rise and one would sink

each of your spirit tongues   incanting worlds of words   that squeeze

this earth   between my time and yours   *weld two centuries' spinal cords in one.*

I'm so far now   from the bench where we've both sat   watching

our motherland unthaw   grow softer like a woman

take its fertile springtime shape: purple

flecks of lilacs   glint off defrosting waters   and snow-drops

carve their way through the unsealing ground   their blue-white bell

blossoms ringing.   Here, on the American plains
I try to hear our histories   rise
but there is only your soft echo: *starving,*   Brother   *like an apple tree*
lagged against winter,   *being senselessly tenderly drawn*   *to another*
bearing generations   of the same sharp stars
piercing yellow

                                through our glaciered skin.

III. To My Father Aleksander

after Pushkin

Along the Dnepr's edge   I heard *the nature of the thirsty land*
and there, you called for me   to reach into the river
with cupped hands   and bring her
to our people's cracking lips.   But on that shore
I sat alone   your voice pressed   between my hands
like this strange flower in this book   and when
I touched the water   it swelled   onto the earth
the steam carrying away your words   over our people's open mouths.

There you first taught me   *Time tends horses to full speed*   and I believed
the way small children do   retreating into rhymes   and holding them
inside my lungs   where *All breathes*

of Rus, the Rus of old.

Still, with broken chestnuts at my foreign feet   I wait for ground
to take the water   I watch the shore recede   and walk
into the river's very throat   I reach the other side
where I could find the shadow   of your body
or traces of its bones   *or maybe*   *they had both faded*   or hid
from stranger's touch   leaving only the poison tree: *Anchar*
standing   *like an awful,*   *silent sentry*
dug into soil and sky   with Russian words I can't recall   or   is it easier
to lie   convince my teeth and tongue   they have forgotten how to speak
deny my eyes   the pages they remember   and let *my voice*
your voice

be still?

Things move slower now   and *poisoned rains*   we never meant to call
pour into scorching sand and stone   from one land to another
both of which   we do not own   silence rises out of vast divide
and from our people's open mouths   horse hooves pound
counting down for your return   to heal the wounded world
unfinished words have   left behind.

IV. To My Country's Bard

after Alexander Rozenbaum

When as a child   I heard your songs   I did not understand
how *gray hands*   could rise out of the water
stretch the channels out towards me   crack the surface
again and again   with *palms where white snow no longer melts*
rise out of the water   *gray*   how could a body turn under the ice
to stone or ashes   and keep on singing   *swimming through*
a human ocean   open mouthed

                    singing

like a fish   *gray*   rise out of the water   become a swallow in the air
while I was still too young to swim or fly with it   but from the ground
I listened   *hear me my dear*   and I listen now   waiting
for bodies to become   music for music   to fall like snow
and all around me   come down your memories
gray   they rise out of the water   *gray*
they tangle with my own

                              I take off my shoes

and search for our wandering people   gather
their floating hands   broken legs
they will strum your gypsy seven-string   they will ride your *gray horse*
among the apples trees in the sky   and dive bareback
into the high-tide of the clouds   they will sing with you
again and again   six million tongues   united in one language
and following their trail of steps and voices   *I'll find my grave*
share the open ground with you   so we hear *the music*
played there so long ago   keeping warm   holding
each other by the hand   we will begin to pray
and our words   will rise so high
                they'll burn the sun.

Epithalamium After 50 Years

A year of marriage counts as three.

—Soviet proverb

Behind us, the Caribbean surf thrums, palm trees clap
their fronds against its wake to dull the edge of familial conversation.

My grandfather raises his shaking glass: *To the way you love your husband!*
He swallows mouthful after mouthful and motions all of us to drink.

His tastes have changed from vodka to cognac to red Chilean wine
he gulps as though this drink could be his last. In 1962, after three tries

he made it clear: *I'll never ask again.* So grandmother said *yes*
because *he wouldn't drink or fight or cheat or raise his voice.*

She liked his quiet manner of pursuit, that only one hand
could make a fist (he'd lost three fingers as a boy). Lost too, his ancestry

during the war; she liked that hers would have to be his own.
They married in the only way they could: a courthouse wedding

with a Ukrainian shawl spread out beneath their feet, a world
woven between them, salt and bread for luck, no rabbi or vows,

and only one picture. She's captured there against him, her eyes
near-closed, in half-sleep maybe. His arm wraps her shoulder firmly,

under his grip, shadows of her skin giving in (the hip would have been
too forward) and her linen dress is wrinkled and yellowed by light or time

or their early means. Together, they weathered: fifty summer swims
under an aging sun, until it grew too dark to see each other's movements

underwater; thirty Soviet snows when the trollies and buses wouldn't run
and he walked her three miles to the night shift, sat waiting on a snow bank

to take her home; nineteen years in a country that stayed foreign,
    where their bodies
became immigrants to one another; three languages (none of which
    were home):

Shut your mouth!
        Xvatit' Lyubanka.
(silence)
        You know your mother always hated me.
Goteniyu tayer! Again?
        I'm not the idiot you make me out to be.
She's dead now. Miortvoya!
        But you still love her more.

They raised two children; took one pilgrimage to the Holy Land
and one to the promised where they found a house with room enough

to sleep alone, him on their queen, her on the foldout, so tradition
looked unchanged. Now, they vacation with the family on annual

lush white beaches and request a room with two beds, waking
hours apart and lying under separate umbrellas, staring far beyond
    the horizon

where sky and ocean blend to an indiscernible blue, a thing
               they both called *beautiful* once.

Under the bed, the monsters grow restless.

Babushka tells me she hasn't been sleeping well,
blames it on old age, a bad duvet cover,

the dreams. *I've been searching*, she says, *for the last
hour. Do you know how hard it is*

to find one that will fit right? Their bed
is small, *So many choices!* And has been

ever since we emigrated. She likes it
that way, the same size as where

there was no option

for a bigger one. *The other night, I was thrashing
so hard,* she must have thrown herself

against my grandfather. *Dedushka had to
wake me.* He must have been so shocked

by such a touch. Must have woken
afraid too. I ask who she was running from.

I rarely remember. It's all such silliness,
she tells me, repeating

she has no idea

where they all come from. *I'm always
trapped, trying to get out. Always failing.*

But last night, *We had a child with us,
age six, I think,* (me the night we left?)

and they were shooting, bandits, shooting.
And again, trapped. She keeps repeating

how it all comes

out of nowhere. *No way out. The shooting*
everywhere. And I keep trying to escape. Repeating

there's no reason for it. These dreams.
Old age. How she doesn't understand.

When you dream

of monsters, I tell her, you know they come
from stories. From childhood. You know

they cannot hide under your bed, inside
your closet, but she checks there, nightly, grateful

not to remember,

most mornings, at least.
Grateful, this past

isn't hers.

And she believes it. *There's so much*
online now. More beds and monsters, more

covers that don't fit well or hide enough.
But how do I choose without touching, without feeling

the fabric? She believes in a softer linen,
believes that it will help her sleep.

After the Stars Fell

It slipped down the side of the sky,
passing by the other stars in its course.

Oscar Wilde, *The Star-Child*

I. February 15, 2013

We heard the risen, ragged sun caught fire:
first, a shadow charcoaled over Chelyabinsk
and turned the air to gunpowder, then
a constellation of ignited smoke
cinched onto clouds and swam across the sky—
foreign rock transformed to shining yellow
walleye, shedding its molten scales of gold
over the unsuspecting, frozen ground.
We missed it all: the shattered glass and panic,
the 'end of days' written in Russian
blood on snow, the moment when the whole
of earth enclosed onto herself, begged us
to let her go. We used to read "Old Earth
is dead," not knowing that the sky would fall.

II. Dream, 1993

Instead of sky, there lies a sleeping black
between the clouds. I'm lost there in uncharted
dark. Sometimes, I am a ship with ghosts
for sails in waves of dying galaxies,
and other times, I'm body floating up
towards Cepheids, blinking blue ignited worlds
like newborn eyes' first waking, forever
barely out of reach. To dream of falling
is the dream. To wake in flight. On fire.
Because I find a secret home in this,
unseen: the reaching, the return. Twenty years
ahead, the dust of our white dwarf falls
soft, soft as new snow, my mother says. But
in my hands, our star melts down to ashes

III. Fortuneteller's Story-Song to My Parents, Timeless

Their question: why's our child awake at night?

> The reading: she dreams her histories, dark,
> unresolved past lives. Look how "The Hanged Man"
> stands, not hovers, ankle roped in solid air,
> he demands, you wait. And cards reversed
> won't lie: the sky does not forgive abandonment.

Wait? For what? Is there nothing we can do?

> Give her back. Lift her to the stars she left.
> Or, one of you can take her darkness,
> carry it. Song and story and night.

But all across the world the stars have fallen.
We have no place when most are orphan,
and all the rest are calling, calling out
for light: child-kings to rise out of the dust.

IV. Sky in May, Today

All are out. Corvus: failed crow, thrown up
for the sky to swallow whole; Virgo: maiden-
mother, setting all her children-lights aglow;
Musca: bright, unnoticed housefly; and
Centaurus, half-man, half-beast, so wounded,
he earned a place among the heavens.
I know them by their history, the way
a heritage is known, so when they stray
from home, go dark, I'll find them, like a part
of flesh, a sureness felt for during sleep.
This far outside the city, night reaches
the ground. The buried touch the burning and
exchange their fairytale for flight, only
to find a place among uncertain stars.

V. Childhood, Year Unknown

Remember the night the power went out:
Papa balancing atop the skeleton
of an un-built house, reaching for the sky?
Recall the worry: would he find his way
or fall, body glowing against the dark
like that child who fell out of the sky but
never came home again? For calm, you sang
of gypsy fortune tellers fanning cards
across their velvet shawls like universes
they could map and trace and understand.
Look how they shape the future out of suns
beside a campfire that won't die down?
Mother, sing me the story of that night.
I only remember the lack of light.

III IN THE FIRE

If you wake up in a world of ashes
remember you have reached God
in your own way.

—Luisa Muradyan, "Cremation"

It must have been the season of the midnight sun,

the ides of July those fifty years ago, when
my grandmother split wide, unbroken, unnamed
light pouring out of her: a river into a river.

Svet: luminescence, shine. The child took a while
to cry. *Sveta:* pure, blessed, divine. The girl
had a weak spine and bowing legs and hardly

any hair and left too little of herself inside.
Call her *Svetlana.* Call her by way of ignited sky
yellow luster and the morning. Know her name

was cast out of orthodox holy water
under the glow of a golden cross. Recast her
chosen and a *zhid* and watch her suffer

the way all light must, knowing
$\qquad\qquad\qquad\qquad\qquad$ it is the light.

For Likht in Soviet Winter

The first time I got coins, my father
made me keep it secret, made me
choose a chocolate gift and
take my time with choosing

how to keep it secret
from the store clerk and my mother,
who took her time with choosing
which candles wouldn't glow

bright enough for the store clerk
to know the origin of light
came from our candles' glow
behind dishtowel curtains

the first time I got coins. My father
believed in something then:
choosing a chocolate gift to teach me
the secret origin of light.

Potatoes Don't Have Much to Do with Light

Frying them up and singing,
      I teach my son
our people are scattered
      seeds and wax-drops clinging
to every surface fire has left
      immune to flame,
Blessed are You, Baruch atah,
      he eats too many to count,
Adonai Eloheinu, golden and dripping
      with sunflower oil and soaked
in apples, though potatoes
      have little to do
with stealing fire from the gas stove,
      Sovereign of all, and carrying it
on my fingertips, *Melech haolam,* to the candles
      in the window, but everything
to do with the season of killing
      ducks, so that their rendered fat
can be found in any house
      along with a forgotten
December onion,
      who hallows us, along with light
enough for eight evenings,
      asher kid'shanu b'mitzvotav,
and at midnight, my son
      exhales an entire latke and is afraid
of what his body leaves behind,
      so he clings to me like wax,
all night refusing his bed,
      all night burrowing
all thirty pounds of him
      into my bones, *commanding us*
to kindle, v'tsivanu l'hadlik
      and in the morning, *ner shel,*
when he is extinguished enough

to stay in his own room, I wake
to find him surrounded in white—
          Tylenol, ibuprofen, Band-Aids,
gauze, the first-aid kit I thought
          was out of reach, scattered
across the floor like a harvest
          of winter potatoes,
and his swollen belly, aglow
          with all our people's
burning starch.

Naming the Flame

after Maeve Shearlaw's "Dropping in on Turkmenistan's 'door to hell'—in pictures"

—The Guardian, July 2014

It has burned as long as Jews
      wandered the desert and longer
           than its home has been a country.

40 years in the middle of nothing,
      burning for nothing and no one,
           spreading nowhere and growing

only in years—a sprawling ephemera
      across the Karakum. A kindling
           contained like desire or

its opposite. An unsealable,
      un-human wound. Like a moth's
           heart or its imagined mouth

trying to swallow the blaze.
      Geography will call it
           the Darvaza Crater.

Science and fiction, the "door
      to hell," and one wingless explorer
           —grounded Icarus, I call him—

names it "coliseum of fire," ignited
      theater of flesh. He stands on its edge
           as though walking into the sun.

He burns
      nothing
           like a body.

Fire, Fire,

my son calls out, imagines flame, light
shooting from his hands, *Fire mountain.*

His hands—*My boat is swimming through fire*—
always unscathed. My great-great-grandmother

burned her whole right side when a vat
of boiling *chenokorka*—black-rind, cherry

preserves—spilled over her skirted thigh, ate
right through the fabric. I imagine her hands

swimming through fire—sugar and pits—clearing
skin of char. Her daughters would grow

afraid of boiling, never bring red fruit
to the stove again. *Fire, Fire,* my son singes

the air with open palms and asks if I see it.
My great-grandfather must have burned too,

though none of us saw those flames either.
My boat, Fire, Fire, falling fire.

When our people's bodies

rose too high—*My mountain, Fire*—the Germans
or Russians or Ukrainians—anyone

without ashes in their blood—discovered
burning always makes more room.

They named the dead

a waste of space inside the earth, my ancestors,
a certain waste above it. But burned, we became

fertilizer—compressed or blown away—lingering
in soil and air—eternal, unnoticed—

in my son's hands—*Fire, Fire.*

Away from Babi Yar

They will never come for citizens like us,
Zahar would say, while most of Kyiv fled
far west into unarmored steppes.

His family stayed to watch him polish
citrine and amber rings, display them
in his storefront, and sell them to the few

remaining Russian wives who refused
to show they'd turned to widows.
By September 1941, the soldiers too

came for the jewels; they dressed
the family in gold, and walked them
glowing through the streets

where a crowd had gathered:
a city of stone in lines of beryl stars.
The father and mother, dark, precise

features, wealthless now, were set in rows
behind others who looked the same,
but their daughter was light enough to slip

yellow off of her dress. *You don't belong*
with dirty Zhids! spoke a medaled man, his gun
pointed beyond where she could see.

Rayachka! Her father's words flew up
like bits of earth as she began to fade
farther from that name. *Where are you going?*

His echo slapped against her nape—
the strike of dirt over a Jewish coffin
with the back of a shovel blade:

courtesy to the dead, a reluctance
to let them go. She disappeared, calling,
I will be right back. Her faint reply

just hovered in the dust.

How to Survive a Heat Wave in Auschwitz

1. Hire uniformed Germans—
   Volkswagen interns—to replace
   barbed wire so it doesn't show
   the wear of winter or tourism.

2. Ask visitors to guess how many
   thousands it took to collect
   the rooms full of hair & tooth-
   brushes & suitcases & names. Wait
   until they fail to see object
   as body. Then, tell them that hair
   doesn't go through preservation
   & will decay someday
   like bone.

3. Let crowds gather at the gates & listen
   to them push their way inside, "Come on,
   it's Auschwitz! Everybody wants
   to get in," one yells in English.

4. Mark each group
   with different colored stickers
   signifying tour-guide language
   & disregard the irony of walls
   displaying triangles & stars—different
   colors signifying type & race & likelihood
   of being counted or remembered.

5. Put up ice cream & snack vendors
   just outside the entrance to encourage
   family picnics on the manicured lawn
   & invite a father to carry his two-year-old
   down into the cells of block 11—where I
   could barely breathe—& allow a mother
   to line her children up

against the reconstructed death wall
for a photo & again under the words
"Arbeit macht frei" & later still a family-
selfie with a crematorium & gas chamber
backdrop. Leave the ashes
cropped out.

6. But don't turn on *the mist showers*
    placed near the facilities' entrance
    to make the visit more pleasant
    on one of the hottest days of the year.

Human Metonymy: A Tour Guide through I and II

The sky is seething
and it starts
to drizzle.

      "For the first two years, prisoners were Polish."
      "Here you can see real human ashes."
      "The average life of a woman was 3-4 months."

Mid-July. Humid.

      "1 crematorium was inefficient."
      "A man lasted 8 months to a year."

There are children
everywhere.

      "1.1 million Jews deported, 90% died."
      "1.5 million visitors come to hear this every year.
          Can you imagine?"
      "Auschwitz II-Birkenau is 20 times bigger.
      Not brick, but wood."

Headphones
are not
just available.
They're required.

      "7 villages leveled to the ground so the camp
          could be built."
      "Established with the goal of killing
          90 thousand people at once."
      "In our collection, there are more than 100,000 shoes."

Someone
is mowing
the lawn.

      "No pictures allowed. Only in this block."
      "How much do you think is here?"

[   ]

      "2 tons of hair. 40 thousand people."

A guard walks by
under a black
umbrella.

        "This is a real train car."

A woman struggles
to push a baby stroller
across wet mulch.

        "Of course we can go inside the gas chamber."

Bicycle baskets, wicker
and full of flowers
pass by along
the other side
of the barbed wire.

        "Do you think they are real?"

[   ]

        "These scratches were made by tourists."

Ruins of Pompeii, or Ancestry

Not whole, the way we know them now, but fragmentary
hollow skeletals that seal the human or reveal
what it once was. Breath stolen by volcanic gas
and corpses dressed in ashes. An imprint of dust
upon the body, or the body onto dust. Excavators filled
the distance between bone and absent skin with plaster,
made flesh-form evident: a naked relic for collection and display.
My grandfather has never been there, but I showed him
pictures of the ageless forms, coiled snails within
a man-made shell: mother and child cinched at the neck
by soot and centuries and history's pressure turning
them diamond. Did he wish then that his mother too
had been cast in immortal ash, or was he grateful
gas chambers, mass graves, and crematoriums left nothing
                                        to reconstruct the body by?

Ghazal Refusing to Name the Holocaust

*After the October 27, 2018 shooting at the Tree of Life—Or L'Simcha
Congregation, Pittsburgh, Pennsylvania*

*Your poetry is so much more relevant now that the Holocaust
is back in fashion,* someone said, because without the Holocaust,

do we not know how to die? To grieve? To lose? To hold each other
against shaking trees? To feel connected by more than the whole cost

of our senseless, constant dying? My babushka would never
tell the story of her husband shot at Babi Yar as Holocaust,

would scream about a Nazi's hands around her neck, his hands
under her skirt, his hands his hands, she would relive the whole accost

of him and never name herself survivor. When Rose was named
eldest among the dead, did the trees not burn? Tear out their roots?
    Holy cost

of dying. When she was named survivor, did you not shake and weep
the same as when they told you she had not survived the Holocaust?

Did you not cling to someone's trunk so hard that it became
a body you could lose, your own arms branching holy, costing

you to fall uprooted. So say their names: Melvin, Irving, Jerry, Cecil, David,
Daniel, Bernice, Sylvan, Joyce, Richard, and Rose. Don't simply name them
                                      Holocaust.

IV IN THE WATER

*If I'm lonely
it's with the rowboat ice-fast on the shore
in the last red light of the year
that knows what it is, that knows it's neither
ice nor mud nor winter light
but wood, with a gift for burning*

—Adrienne Rich, "Song"

Misremembering Stones

We are always afraid. My mother and grandmother say. *Afraid to lose everything.* Their echoing refrain. They want me to live more cautiously. To live as though I'd lost more. *Afraid because everything has been taken away before.* Their fear didn't start out this way. It has grown heavier and more urgent with each year—poppy seed to sunflower to stone, a bone lodged in the throat—because each year brings more that can be lost.

In Ukraine, we had little, but I remember it as always enough. Though tangerines and American candy bars were only for special occasions, and I had to keep secret that I was buying them with Hanukkah gelt, I'd never known my grandfather's starvation or father's bloodied Jewish nose or the stones they'd both placed on unmarked earth beneath which their missing ancestors might lie.

Once though, I was teased for being the *zhid* girl. The neighborhood boys threw stones. My parents don't remember this. Maybe the memory isn't mine or isn't a memory even. Maybe it's part of the mythology written for my short-lived Soviet childhood—floating amid hours waiting for bread and walking atop rusted fountains when the Dnepr flooded and watching women move through our tiny kitchen with its bathtub doubling as a table when covered by a wooden board and eating hot persimmons ripened on the radiators and knowing someone was always at the stove, the flame always lit.

Maybe it's something I've chosen to claim, so I too have the loss my family passes down. So my un-accented English is tinged with our refugee-immigrantness. So I remember that here, I am being passed as a white woman, while across the Atlantic, whiteness washes away and I'm that little girl I imagine, everything to fear and little to lose.

Let the father give

the first bath, the midwife instructed
but not until the wound

has healed. Wait   *at least ten days*
before washing, before breaking

his face away from skin. *He's not*
unclean, she explained

my son's waxy coating—*vernix*
caseosa, filament my body left, a gift

of second skin—protects
against infection—group B strep,

E. coli, distance, other common
pathogens. *We're going to separate*

your kids   *so they can bathe,*
the agent instructed at the border—

the children not seen again.
How washing can make the body

disappear—
naked, bald,

my son looked less than
human that first time—

rising just above the water's
touch   shock

at something other than
my body, perhaps knowing

in his bones
dirt washes away

as easily   as skin.
His father's hands

worked gentle, slow,
to reassure him   of return.

Things the river forgets:

that it is water,   moving and   unmoved

its refusal   to ask   about the blood

that my grandfather walked into its mouth and nearly drowned

        when the current rose to his knees

that he swallowed sand and heard it   crack his lungs

that at the surface   core and corpse and corporal   can't be

        ground to coriander

that we too are made of seeds

its own image flowing powder   out of our hands

his body is not as heavy as it was once

bones   hollow as a seagull's

the little left will wash up on these banks in swaths

jellyfish that tried   to live in freshwater   but winter's current

        carried them to salt   and spit them back out

that he was quiet   quiet underwater   when a child

        pulled him out

an ungraspable fish

that he wasn't   in a river   at all

that the sea is just a mouth

                –full of rivers

Rust

Bridges have fallen from less.
And boats   bicycles   train tracks   the buckle
on our suitcase   the grinder gears beneath
my grandfather's left hand.
I want to know more
about your past, I said to him
over dessert. *Yeah? Me too.* He looked away and picked
at something stuck between his teeth, used
the pointer finger on the hand that still has one.
It must have smelled of iron then, the gap
between his thumb and pinky where
the blade churned bone where oxygen and water ran
nine stiches   maybe ten   a bridge between the palm and dorsal
skin never meant to meet the other side of skin.
He's never told me how it happened.
I don't know   how to ask.
He hasn't starved in decades, but that's all he wants
to tell me.   Hunger   birds   searching for bread
boys searching   for birds searching   for bread
onions in oil   brined fish   a potato, maybe   certainly,   always
potatoes   no yeast   no fruit   an onion
serves as both   and bridges have fallen   without it
and no one   lifted a finger   or noticed.
He likes to retell the first time
he thought he saw a mandarin.
Its porous ocher shell giving way
under the pressure of his touch,
the orb so big and singing, he could barely wrap it
in all ten fingers. *It was like holding*
the sun. He said and cupped the air.

I don't ask when he could last interlace
the fingers on both hands and pray
for citrus. But maybe our sun really is
surrounded by a solid iron surface.
As grandfather bit down into the rind,
he must have tasted solar flares
until he heard somebody laugh.
The lemon's oil turned acid rust
against his tongue, left only iron, the last
refusing to collapse when a star dies.

Translating Grandfather's Hunger

I

He barely speaks English. When he tries to say *how are you?* it comes out as *hava you? хаваю!* In Russian, to gobble or eat with a fury. And this, he does. First, a plate full of salad with lettuce overflowing onto the floor by the time he makes it back to the table from the buffet line. Next, red meat and baked potatoes and seared fish and some grilled vegetables covered by some rotisserie chicken and mysterious sauces. And when it comes time for dessert, he has two separate dinner plates, one with a leaning tower of fruit and the other, a mountain of pastries and cakes and at least two scoops of ice cream, vanilla usually, though anything made of milk and sugar will do. And tea, always tea. *Chamomile, two bags,* Babushka instructs the waiter, even if Dedushka would have preferred something else. He never lets it steep long enough before drinking, takes in the bitter hot water as close to boiling as he can get.

II

How are you feeling?

I call during my walk   along the ten-minute stretch   between dropping
his great-grandson at daycare and arriving   at the coffee shop to write this.
I was reading   Speigleman's MAUS. I'm sure it has something to do with this,
I think.   Guilt and the pressure   of time or its lack.   Before, I would only call him
by mistake. He has so little   to say these days.

          Oy   Nechego

          literally meaning   nothing   but colloquially   the word   for fine

Not nothing, not fine. You just exclaimed Oy. Is it your legs?

          Yes. It's my legs.

          he refuses surgery   people die in hospitals   he says

Have you gone on your walk already today?

This autumn light in early October is beyond   description.
I imagine he wore at least three layers.
Being cold is not   something he has to bear   anymore.
He keeps the condo hot.   Wears his jogging suit indoors.
Babushka sneaks the windows   open. She even insisted   he take off
his sweater so we could break   fast. She didn't let him   eat the soup.
He'd already had two bowls   full   some two hours earlier.

And what are your plans for the day?

          Your grandmother left me things to do. Vacuum. Wash floors.
          She always   leaves me   tasks.

Good that she is keeping you busy. I want to keep you busy too.
Tell me about the past.

The last time I asked in person, said I wanted to know   more. He said
he did too.   Wanted   to know that is.

About your childhood.

          What childhood?

Well, what's the first thing you remember?

          The first thing, I didn't go *v sadik*
          to the small garden   children's garden   kindergarten
          I stayed home and I was hungry.

Did they feed you at kindergarten?

Yes, there they fed us.

Why were you home?

I was confused already.

I was sick. I didn't go *v sadik* because I was sick. I was home
so I was hungry. I wanted food. So I went there to get food
even though I was sick.

Were you home alone.

*How did he get there?   Where was his mother? Brother?   I am always afraid
to ask about his father. Papa makes him stop talking.   Food   does the opposite.*

Yes. Mama was always working. I was hungry. Always.

How old were you?

I don't know. Young. Not old enough to be in school yet.

Five. Maybe six. Seven?

What were you sick with?

I don't remember. I was hungry.

Do you remember what they fed you at kindergarten?

No.

*I thought he always remembered   food. The lemon   he mistook
for an orange. The giant   peaches that grew   only in the south.
The empty cabinets and pantry.   Not even a potato, he repeats.
Always recalling how Babushka's mother never let her children starve.
Always onions and oil and salted   fish at least
the onions.   Always   something to chew.*

We were in Samarkant, Uzbekistan then. In evacuation.

What else do you remember?

I was sick and I had to go *v sadik* because I was hungry.

Well I have to go now.

*I needed to read   someone else's story.   He sounded tired.
But he always sounds   tired   when he talks now.*

Try to remember more of your past. I will call later
and ask you about it. It will help me   if you remember.

I know he is more likely to do it if it's for someone else.

It's good for your health to remember.

Maybe that's a lie.

Thank you.

He doesn't add   for calling.   He is always grateful
when I accidentally call   him.

III

He doesn't speak Yiddish, but sings all the words to *Tumbala Laika,* likely recalling songs of a father he never knew. He doesn't speak Spanish either, but still says *como estas?* and expects an answer from anyone who looks to him like his amigos at the resorts in Mexico, where he can eat unstoppably, for every meal, especially if Babushka is too busy with a great-grandchild to notice. One time, too many years ago now, he asked the landscapers working on the beach for their ladder and climbed a coconut tree to get the fruit down. Then, he had them drill holes in the thick brown shell so he could feed us fresh milk. Once we'd sucked that dry, he used one of their axes to split the sphere in two so we could scoop out flesh and know what it's like to hold that tender sweetness on our tongues against the sun's beating and the saltwater's approach. I still wonder how they understood. How they smiled and slapped each other on the back, Dedushka's skin darker than theirs, his belly bigger, and his mouth, always open.

IV

You sound more upbeat today.

I downloaded an app that will record all of our conversations. Should I tell him?

      Thank you. I just came back from walking.

It's so   _____ out.

The Russian word I used has no translation. Ravishing and gorgeous
and adjectives are too   far from truth.

Where did you go?

      Just walked around the building.

And your legs?

It's so easy to ask about his body.   The answer always certain.
His body anything but.

      Budit' luchshe.

      Literally   will be   better   future indefinite tense

When?

      I don't know. Eventually?

I want to ask about his mother again.   About the hunger.   The past.
His fingers.   Instead

Did Babushka leave you things to do today?

      Yes. Dusting.

I wish you could come here and dust. We have so much dust.

      Sigh   deep   long

      I hope I have enough time to get our house done.

      One bedroom   one bath   apartment on the 6th floor
      balcony looking down   at the parking lot   every now and again
      a bird   pigeon maybe or even a crow

Enough time? What else do you have to do?

I should have asked already. What he remembers. All these things I want
to write down before   time runs out.

He's afraid he might not get all the dust. I'm afraid to ask   why.

      Well now, I'm going to eat.

      And it's back to food.   It starts and ends   in the mouth.

What are you going to have?

I know the answer. It'll be soup. It's always soup.

    Soup.

What kind?

    He can't think of the word   Soup of   *from the brain to the mouth*
    something is lost you know the one   *sigh*   *maybe he's taking*
    off his shoes   Fish   Uxa

Oh, okay then.

I should ask.   *The dust can wait.*   *Soup can wait.*   *Remember, I told you*
to try and remember.   *Did you?*

Well enjoy.

    Thank you. How's your ear. No wait, that wasn't you.

His other granddaughter has an ear infection. He confuses us sometimes.

Good luck with the dust.

This recording on my phone is five and a half minutes long, but I haven't listened.

V

Now, he barely speaks, and when he tries, Babushka finishes his sentences in any language. Missing three fingers on his left hand, Dedushka still has all his teeth and a very able tongue. He has an aptitude for food and language, not memory. An aptitude for eating and feeding and opening his mouth, but there's rarely anyone to translate his ways.

Of Lemons and Skin and Teacups

let's flay it open: find the tea
in tear   and moan   in lemon
the obsession in   the one   obsessed
with sectioning the body   into inside and
the "wordless   thing"   that covers it

—derma   casing   cutis   hull   shell   parch
ment   vellum   peel   film   fell—
let's ask   how different   this severing
and fall: the flesh of man   and fruit
in muted color   in   a teacup   full
of bathwater and salt   and what mistakes
as memory: a stranger's   hands
holding my legs   together:
a lemon   wedged into my gums
as acid sponge   absorbing all
that wild and childhood   screaming

let's forget   that this   fixed nothing:
that the bitter   porous rind   was skin
and always mine   that brewed
too long   tea curdles   on the tongue
that lemons   are less   fruit
than failed or failing   memory:
those skinless   strangers   inside
cup-fulls of tears   steeped down   to tea

Babushka wants us all to take a cruise

because she made her son ride low
       in a cargo ship once when a storm
          slammed against the portholes
             waves crested hounds' teeth
                and lights rattled like scared hands,
because my uncle's small ones couldn't hold
       the acid inside and let it pour out of him,
          because he's been afraid ever since,
             of ships and dogs, because Babushka
                can choose on which deck we'll sleep now,
can buy us a balcony or concierge, can name
       the ships, Summit, Century, Solstice,
          Silhouette, Reflection, Equinox, nothing
             that rings of freight or Soviet, because she refuses
             to retire, but comes home aching
nearly eight decades hanging
       off her spine, living only to do it
          all over again, because of her children,
             because she's spent a third of her life
                in this country and knows
she'll die here, still foreign,
       because she loves
          the way home is possible
             in no one's waters and go years
                without seeing her sister's face,
though they only live twenty minutes
       apart now, *but family*, she tells me,
         is different here, is gone, because
            there is no such thing
              as obligation and I'm complaining
about cost and difficulty, traveling
       with a toddler, *because we hardly had enough*
         underwear for our children, she says,
             because some days, she wanted chocolate
             so badly, but could never spare

a *kopeika,* because she never went hungry,
     even after the war, her mother made sure
          there were always potatoes and onions,
               because these are still
                    her comfort foods, but she can choose
to dip anything in chocolate now, though her stomach
     can't handle seeds or nuts anymore,
          because a week of all-you-can-
               eat-and-drink, together, locked
                    in metal and salt, isn't
too much to ask, because once,
     she called "ship," a "sheep," struggling
          to differentiate the long [ee]
               and short [i] sounds, because now,
                    she can say "shit" and means it,
to describe old age or laxatives or
     my grandfather, because now,
          she must hang a "sheet"
               above the toilet to remind him,
                    "flush," because *I'm not afraid*
to die, she tells me, but shit, she's a bad liar
     and the Atlantic is as good a place as any
          for truth to drown, because
               in the end,
                    all of us float.

Driftwood Pantoum

And in the dream, she was just bones
searching for what holds her together—
a river the width of ten bodies.
Stop closing your eyes, this isn't your story,

searching for what holds her together.
You can't let her rest, my mother says.
Stop closing your eyes, this isn't your story
She's turning in her grave each time you write

not letting her rest, my mother says,
tells me to read about Hitler's last descendants.
She's turning in her grave each time you write this.
They live in long Island and refuse to have children.

There are five of them, Hitler's last descendants—
a river the width of ten bodies.
They live in Long Island and refuse to have children
And in the dream, she is still just bones.

V IN THE ÆTHER

If I speak for the dead, I must leave
this animal of my body,

I must write the same poem over and over,
for an empty page is the white flag of their surrender.

—Ilya Kaminsky, "Author's Prayer"

Against Ritual

The warmth of December snow, a return
to unfinished song: *turning and twisting,*
big blue balloon. Your mind lost long ago

save to taste and sound, senses that brought
you back to a kind of home—chocolate
blinchiki and Russian guitar ballads:

turning and twisting like a giant blue moon.
I should have kept strumming
so you'd clap and sing the wrong words,

your hands and mouth too weak
for such noise. But the day before
you died, *turning and twisting, wanting*

to fall down, you remembered:
man wants to hold his love on the ground.
Remembered everything: where our faces fit

against your palms' lifelines and what names
to call great-grandchild, daughter, ghost husband—
knowing   not to call out

his name. And we thought
you healed. *Where is this street, where is this home?*
Your echo hovering in the room where

I didn't tear off my clothes or cover my body
with ash. I didn't even cover yours—close
the mouth and eyes, hung wide and silent.

Where is this woman that I love alone?
I didn't answer, looking up at you—body
frozen in melodic yawn. I didn't crown your head

with candles and beg forgiveness: *Here is this street,*
here is this home. I didn't stay to watch you shift
into a hollow. I didn't stay to learn the absence of a thing

trying to leave the body. *Here is this woman*
that I love alone: your unsung breath suspended—
teaching me all I'll ever need to know of absence.

Ghost Language

We lied to you that last year. It passed, we'd say or else
you'd do it anyway. Against your body, refuse
to drink and eat and wash, refuse to take the pills.
Refuse our hands. You'd sit there mumbling
in Yiddish, calling quietly for Him as though
he were your husband, *Gotteniu tiyer, Gotteniu veis mir.*
Call it love or prayer or madness, that language
between dead and living ghosts. *Gotteniu.*
Beloved. The words clung to your mouth,
your lips so dry that year we lied, I did it for you.
As an excuse to starve at first. To thin
closer to bone. To know how skin
wears us. The next year you were dead
and still I kept and keep on starving,
stretching out my hands to feel for ghosts,
for you and him and maybe Him.
Gotteniu. Ghost–God, Ghost–great thing
that ends or begins with father.

Olam Ha-Ba

Nothing like hunger, like the want from its resurfacing
      out of what resembles sleep, not knowing
           where one end. Nothing

like beginning: the wonder—cicada-like—buried
      or forgotten for 13 years, but nothing
           like rebirth, louder and more primal.

Nothing like a soul—bodied or otherwise—
      and is there a difference? Nothing
           like questioning: where do the missing

21 grams go? Why must some eyes sink
      unaided? Why do others need help
           closing? How heavy do they weigh

inside? Nothing like weight: the freedom from it,
      human bones to hollow flight as though
           some godly mouth has blown them full

enough to rise—skin and sin intact. But nothing
      like sin: slow, measured, waiting or willing
           things to change, the seasons,

too mild a metaphor and birth, too harsh, more
      like some animal shifting the color of its coat,
           looking less like itself and more the earth or

nothing like it altogether, walking unchanged
      until *you* stop outside a synagogue and see it
           is nothing like that license plate: "God Loves

You." Fish swim towards another frame: "Real men
      love Jesus!" And it becomes more
           like trying to read a language turned

foreign, to place the "you" that isn't you
within a faithless text, within hunger
that's nothing like hunger, but want for it.

For the lost songs

where the *shiksa* cuts butter
with a meat knife and the *rebbe*
tells you to cover it in ash
set it on fire among the coals
and stick it in the straw earth
to make it Kosher again

where Odessa is a pearl by the black sea
and Kostya brings her scows full
of cephas and at 7:40 she opens
and closes to Jews and you hear

the orphan boy beg in Yiddish
for you to purchase *papirosi*
and the poor girl sells

bublichki because her father
reaches for the vodka and mother
for the dishrag and sister for the man
who pays for her reach and then

the lover blindly repeats
tumbala tumbala tumbalalaika and let's
be happy all the while
wondering if he will
ever be
loved

If Nameless Fields Could Sing

We expected to find it
alone, just us in that sun
under the evergreens
among Zbylitowska Góra's
enclosed grass plots marked
with names and towns
for Poles, left nameless
Hebrew text for Jews.
Instead, we walked into a forest
of flags growing wild
without roots. Young boys
with Magen Davids draped
heavy, blue stripes over white. Boys
with yarmulkes and prayer shawls
and heads covered and arms wrapped
in each other. So many young boys. A few
older ones. A rabbi. Two boys helping
another walk. A disabled boy. And another one. And then
that singing. Singing
                rose like smoke.
                              Dai dai dai

dai dai dai
                          dai dai dai dai.
And one of those boys
                    wailed.   Wailed as the rest sang.
Rocked and wailed. And they surrounded
the site
where children
are said
                    to have been shot.
Nameless and gone. The grass. Wild flowers and bright
butterflies. Neon green and white amid purple blooms.
                           And the flags.
The singing. The wailing. The rocking. The air
heavy with prayer. And a smaller group of girls.

Shoulder to shoulder, dressed in flags too and some
carrying stones and some one another and most
crying and some just standing.
But that boy's wail cut
through huddled bodies.
The boy carried by other boys.
The boy who didn't need
the facts. Who needed
to wail. But we are not
crying or tearing off our clothes
or lighting candles but I wish
we were. Wish I could have joined them.
Sang and swayed and
wailed. Wish that
was what we had come to do. To linger
with the unnamed on their soil. To mourn. But we
came to learn
the facts.
                To know that

                        on the first day 6,000 were shot.
                        2,000 Poles, 8,000 Jews, and at least
                        800 children by the end of the second.

That the monument reads

                        "Polish Citizens"
                        and forgets
                        ethnicity.

We came to know

                        the dates
                        and times
                        and numbers.

To listen. But not to wail.
To hear. But not pray. To learn
without feeling.
To look for light
in the break between the trees,
where evergreens turn black
against the high-noon sun

and wailing becomes song
becomes prayer becomes
all that's left of god.

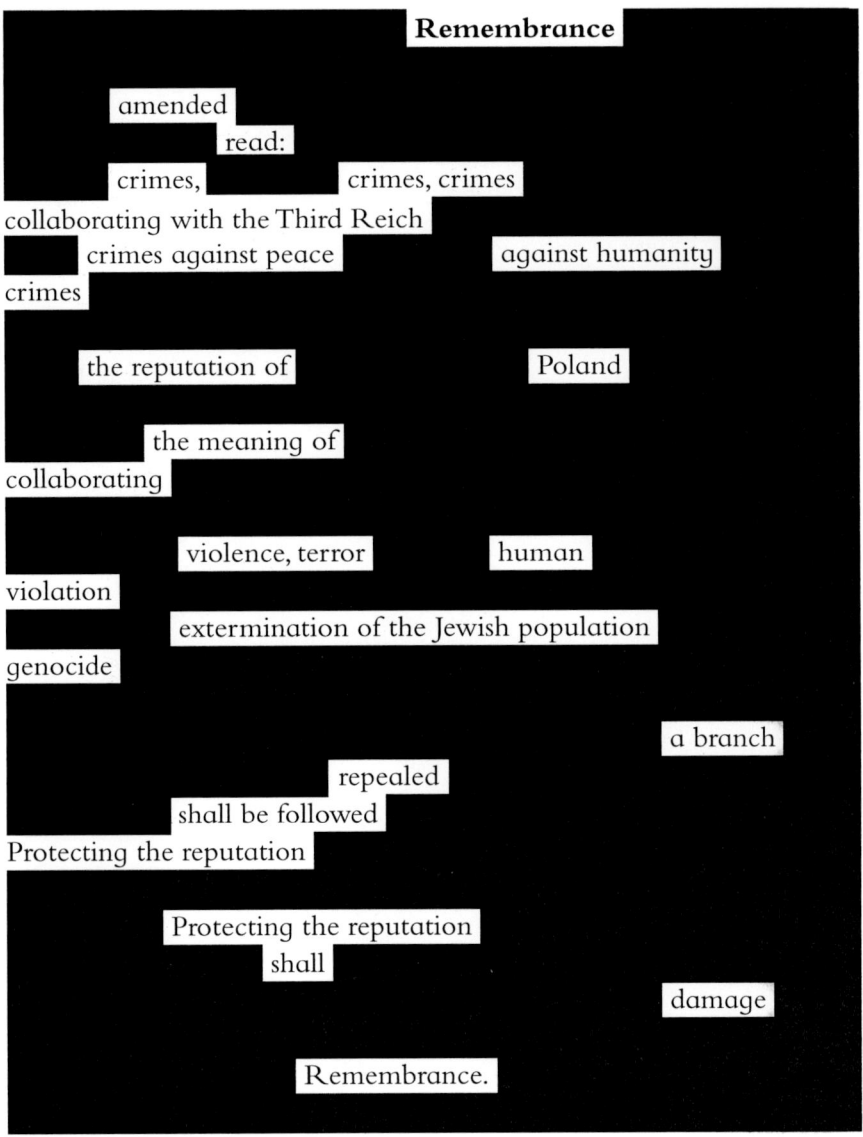

Remembrance

amended

read:

crimes,   crimes, crimes

collaborating with the Third Reich

crimes against peace   against humanity

crimes

the reputation of   Poland

the meaning of

collaborating

violence, terror   human

violation

extermination of the Jewish population

genocide

a branch

repealed

shall be followed

Protecting the reputation

Protecting the reputation
shall

damage

Remembrance.

Note: Poland's 2018 law states: "Whoever claims that the Polish Nation is responsible or co-responsible for Nazi crimes committed by the Third Reich . . . shall be liable to a fine or imprisonment for up to three years." The poem is an erasure of the law's text.

rash, Shaye, 1871, Leova, Romania, Place of death unknown | Barash, Shaul, Tsibulevka, Ukraine (USSR), Murdered in Obodu own | Barash, Sheindl, Hancesti, Romania, Place of death unknown | Barash, Sheindl, 1912, Chmalnik, Pola a, Ukraine (USSR) | Barash, Sheindl, Leovo, Romania, Place of death unknown | Barash, Sheindl, Leova, Roman (USSR), Place of death unknown | Barash, Shifra, Galicia Region, Poland, Place of death unknown | Barash, Sheyad lace of death unknown | Barash, Shlema, 1916, Yemilchino, Ukraine (USSR), Murdered in Yemilchino arash, Shlima, 1881, Starokonstantinov, Ukraine (USSR), Murdered in Starokonstantinov, Ukraine (USSR) 878, Starokonstantinov, Ukraine (USSR), Murdered in Starokonstantinov, Ukraine (USSR) | Barash, Shloma : (USSR), Place of death unknown | Barash, Shlomo, Place of death unknown | Barash, Shtoja eath unknown | Barash, Shmuel, 1925, Kamionka, Poland, Murdered in Galicia Region, Poland | Barash ilonka Strumilowa, Poland, Place of death unknown | Barash, Shoshana, 1895, Khisinau, Romania, Murdered

Barash, Simon, 1909, Kyiv .... Place of death unknown.

n | Barash, Sioma, 1928, Luginy, Ukraine (USSR), Murdered in Luginy, Ukraine (USSR) | Barash, Sona, ya, Poland, Place of death unknown | Barash, Somya, Volkovysk, Poland, Place of death unknown | Barash, land, Murdered in Korec, Poland | Barash, Sonya, Volkovysk, Poland, Place of death unknown | Barash, nionka, Poland, Murdered in Kamionka, Poland | Barash, Sosha, 1922, Kamionka Strumilowa, Poland, ind | Barash, Srul, Lutsk, Poland, Murdered in Lutsk, Poland | Barash, Srul, 1896, Leova, Romania, Murdered irash, Syoma, Khmelnik, Ukraine (USSR), Place of death unknown | Barash, Tanya, 1925, Striyevn, Ukraine d in Striyevo, Ukraine (USSR) | Barash, Tatyana, 1923, Novograd Volynsk, Ukraine (USSR), Murdered in sk, Ukraine (USSR) | Barash, Teibel, Dawid Grodek, Poland, Murdered in Dawid Grodek, Poland | Barash, rodek, Poland, Place of death unknown | Barash, Tila, 1903, Tet, Hungary, Murdered in Auschwitz, Poland | 022, Lodz, Poland, Murdered in Auschwitz, Poland | Barash, Tova, 1919, Lodz, Poland, Murdered in Auschwitz, th, Tvi, 1891, Place of death unknown | Barash, Tzal, Kiev, Ukraine (USSR), Murdered in Babi Yar | Barash, ... | Barash, Tzipora, Khotin, Romania, Place of death unknown | ..... Stojanow, Poland, Place of death unknown ...... Velvl, Khmelnik, Ukraine

I. Horizon

an accumulation	*or physical place:*
buttons on his shirt	everywhere
bits of cloth eaten away	the ashes fell
a photo of his daughter	for all we know
but no, she was too young	it might have been summer
such light	and in the heat
some kind of weapon	his body stinking
small enough to hide in trees	in the forest where even currants
his bones his bones his bones	refused to grow

II. Nadir

from the French archif
"records   or documents preserved"

                              the photo she never got
                              to give him, *На память*
                              (to memory or remember
                              me by) is inscribed,
                              Симочке, От лучшего
                              друга и товарища (from
                              your best friend and companion)
                              Веры, Vera or Faith, *Август,* 17, 1937

from Late Latin *archivum* (plural *archiva*)
"*written   records*"

Семён/Симочка/Cemon/Semon/Сеня
/Senya/Сима/Sima/Симха/Simcha/Симон
Simon/сёма/sioma/муж/husband/отец/
/father/папа/дед/дедушка/grand
father/прадедушка/great-grandfather
/great-great-grandfather/пра-пра-
дедушка/великий/great/dead/
deceased/gone/shot/dead/murdered/dead
/пропавши без вестей/missing/dead/
without a trace/dead/without news/
dead/without birds/dead/dyed/dedushka

III. Zenith

from *arkhe*
"government,"   *literally "beginning, origin, first place"*
his daughter must call   her older sister to find out
the exact date he was born.   Her father.
Year of death assumed.   Death itself as certain
as birth. City?   *Kyiv, I think,*
Babushka   writes in an email.
I'm making   an archive.
Their words about him.   I imagine
he was quiet.

IV. Meridian

also "to rule, lead the way, govern, rule over, be leader of" a word of uncertain origin.

each day, sometime between rising and setting, the sun
will cross the place of his body, when it is highest,
his bones, will be warmed, when it is lowest, the sun
will touch him the way the earth does, the way we dream of

VI IN THE BODY

To stand, in the shadow
of a scar in the air

Stand-for-no-one-and-nothing.
Unrecognized,
for you
alone.

With all that has room within it,
even without
language.

—Paul Celan, translated by John Felstiner

Bone Appendix

after Alexandra Petrova

Trace your son's left hand
      against construction paper
            with a non-toxic marker,

      teaching him the edges
of his bones. Then fill
      the space between

         with what shines
      or powders, glitter,
crushed cheerios, even

      flecks of skin, teaching him
         his bones remain
      in spite of it. Let him

try to fit his fingers
      in the contours,
         tomorrow or

      the next day, teaching him
his bones keep growing.
      And when he makes

         two fists, afraid
      his body can't keep up
with what's inside,

      clenching hard as teeth
         to keep his bones
      just as they are, to keep them

from sprouting out, tell him
      of the oldest Ukrainian apple tree
            that grows its branches

      low into the ground
until they drink the soil—
      an indiscernible colony

            of roots or eternally new trees.
      And when he's falling
asleep pressed to your chest,

      trace his right hand
            against the tree-house
      ribcage it first grew, teaching him

the endlessness of bones.

Phalanx Bone Shehecheyanu

Praise these   your fingers   their tiny bones   each one
a tooth   a needle   a loosening and reach
named for how far they grow   away from you
for their distance from your other bones   from
your body   or mine   the one closest
to your palm   proximal   phalanx
a surrender   a shield   the subsequent
a phalange   something   I can't understand
like your pinky toe   too small
to lodge inside my heart   but there it is
the smallest part of you   forever there
keeping time and beating   you laugh and push
your whole foot in my mouth   how funny
that it fits there   so completely   that you love
knowing it has a home inside   then
the middle bone and distal one   together
they are everything your hands can hold
and everything your feet may tread on
together   they are everything   I'm made of
bone of my bone   blood of mine and not mine
praise   praise   these   your tiny bones
they are the what god must have meant   with every exhale

Acknowledgments

Thank you to the editors of the following publications where these poems first appeared.

The Account: A Journal of Poetry, Prose, and Thought: "How to Survive a Heat Wave in Auschwitz" and "Ghazal Refusing to Name the Holocaust"
The Adroit Journal: "Potatoes don't have much to do with light"
American Poetry Journal: "Hyoid Bone Kaddish" (Reprint)
Anomaly: "If Nameless Fields Could Sing"
Academy of American Poetry: "Out of Stone"
American Poetry Review: "Phalanx Bone Shehecheyanu"
The Bear Who Ate the Stars Chapbook (Split Lip Press, 2014): "Olam Ha-Ba"
Berfrois: "I. February 13, 2013" from "After the Stars Fell"
Gulf Coast: "It must have been the season of the midnight sun,"
Guernica: "Hyoid Bone Kaddish"
Horsethief: "Naming the Flame"
Jewish Currents: "Let the father give"
Lilith Magazine: "Away from Babi Yar"
Lumina: "Against Ritual"
Narrative Magazine: "Family Portrait as a Collection of Bones"
Nashville Review: "Human Metonymy: A Tour Guide through I and II" and "Fire, Fire"
New South: "Translating Grandfather's Hunger"
Poetica Magazine: "Don't touch the bones." and "Driftwood Pantoum"
POETRY Magazine: "Bone Appendix"
Poetry Northwest: "Things the river forgets"
Rattle: "In Praise of Forgetting"
Room Magazine: "Ruins of Pompeii, or Ancestry"
Rust + Moth: "After the Stars Fell"
Southern Humanities Review: "Songs of Home"
Superstitions Review: "Epithalamium After 50 Years"
SWWIM: "Take a piece of earth"
The Southeast Review: "Under the bed, the monsters grow restless"
TriQuarterly: "Of Lemons and Skin and Teacups" and "Rust"

Immense gratitude to Lost Horse Press' Christine Holbert and contest judge Sandra Alcosser for hearing this book and bringing it to readers.

With great appreciation for the following institutions who have supported these poems throughout their various stages: The University of Maryland, The University of Oregon, The University of Pennsylvania, The Yiddish Book Center's Tent: Creative Writing Conference, The United States Holocaust Museum and Memorial (USHMM), The Bread Loaf Writer's Conference, and especially The Auschwitz Jewish Center (AJC). The three weeks I spent in Poland as part of the AJC Fellowship inspired much more than a few poems within this collection, but its larger arc as well as my own understanding of where I fit within an unwitnessed ancestral history.

Gratitude to my multidisciplinary teachers and mentors in the fields of creative writing, Holocaust studies, and literature: Michael Collier, Geri Doran, Al Filreis, Annette Finley-Crosswhite, Judith Greenberg, Kathryn Hellerstein, Elana Jankel, Tomek Kuncewicz, Jo Park, Kevin M.F. Platt, Paul Saint-Amour, Shiri Sandler, Anya Krugovoy Silver, Anika Walke, Liliane Wiessberg, and Maciek Zabierowski. To Jehanne Dubrow for a forward that so beautifully and profoundly situates this book within the larger body of writing about the Holocaust. To Garrett Hongo for the mentorship that let my poetry sing and the foreword that hears its song.

To the poets I am lucky to call friends, who have been there as readers and supporters throughout the writing and rewriting of these poems. Thank you for your eyes and ears: Tina Mozelle Braziel, Sara Rebeka Burnett, Chen Chen, Flower Conroy, Luke Hollis, Steven Kleinman, Cate Lycurgus, Jenna Lynch, Luisa Muradyan, sam sax, Carl Swart, Kelly Grace Thomas, Sam Herschel Wein, Ross White, Alexis Zimberg, and Maya Jewell Zeller.

To the baristas at Ultimo Coffee on 22nd and Catherine—where most of this manuscript was composed—thank you for fueling my writing with the best extra-hot lattes. And to Taylor Engel, my dear friend, thank you for all the baby holding and child entertaining while I wrote or sipped.

To my husband, my love, thank you for always understanding the time away from family writing requires and never letting me feel guilty for it. Thank you for making me feel loved and appreciated every day, for being the most devoted father, and for making my family's story yours too.

To my family, Svetlana S., Michael, Simon, and Dmitry Kolchinsky, Rita Barash, and Vikhlya Khalfin, thank you for sacrificing everything to immigrate to the United States, where I could find my voice. Thank you for such unconditional, interminable love. To my Mama, thank you for raising me on the Russian poets whose music inspired my own and for your unfaltering belief in my words. To my Papa, Dedushka, Uncle, Babushka, and Pra-Babushka, thank you for your stories, they sing from these pages.

And to my children, Valen and Remy—Val'ushka and Remichka—thank you for teaching me that no matter the losses of our past, the future, your future my little loves, is boundless. You are living memory and light.